MW01205027

© 2002 by Barbour Publishing, Inc.

ISBN 1-58660-440-6

Cover art © Photodisc, Inc.

Viola Ruelke Gommer contributed to selections on pages 14, 16, 32, 34, and 38.

Scripture quotations marked NLT are taken from the *Holy Bible*, New Living Translation, copyright © 1996. Used by permission of Tyndale House Publishers, Inc. Wheaton, Illinois 60189, U.S.A. All rights reserved.

Published by Barbour Books, an imprint of Barbour Publishing, Inc., P.O. Box 719, Uhrichsville, Ohio 44683
www.barbourbooks.com

Printed in China.

I'M GLAD WE'RE
Friends

ELLYN SANNA

Friends are an indispensable part
of a meaningful life.
They are the ones who share
our burdens and multiply our blessings.

BEVERLY LAHAYE

I'm glad we're friends because. . .

- I know I can depend on you.
- You nourish my soul and enrich my life.
- You are my soul mate.
- You were my yesterday friend, and I know you will be my tomorrow friend as well.

Friendship is something that
raises us almost above humanity. . . .
It is the sort of love one can imagine between angels.

C. S. LEWIS

1

I Can Depend on You

What would I do without you?
When I need to complain to someone. . .
when I want to share a joy. . .
when I'm discouraged and sad. . .
when I'm feeling silly and want to laugh. . .
you're always there.
I depend on your presence in my life.
Thank you!

A friend is one to whom one may pour out all of the contents of one's heart, chaff and grain together, knowing that the gentlest of hands will take and sift it, keep what is worth keeping, and with a breath of kindness, blow the rest away.

ARABIAN PROVERB

Friendship, like the immortality of the soul, is too good to be believed. When friendships are real, they are not glass threads or frost work, but the solidest things we know.

RALPH WALDO EMERSON

Life needs a structure, a framework, a foundation. Otherwise, all the events and circumstances would tumble into chaos.

Talking with you, sharing our lives, you help me sort through my life and find that sense of solid order. Life no longer seems like a jumble of happenstance. Your words and actions point me toward the eternal meaning that's hidden at life's center.

I'm glad we're friends.

Life is fortified by many friendships.

SYDNEY SMITH

❧

Your presence in my life strengthens me.
I rely on your understanding,
your concern, your laughter, and your prayers.
I am stronger because of you.

Friendship is the allay of our sorrows,
the ease of our passions,
the discharge of our oppressions,
the sanctuary to our calamities,
the counselor of our doubts,
the clarity of our minds,
the emission of our thoughts,
the exercise and improvement of what we meditate.

JEREMY TAYLOR

It is sublime to
feel and say of another,
. . . I rely on him as on myself.

RALPH WALDO EMERSON

2

You Nourish
My Soul
and Enrich
My Life

You and I have experienced joy and sorrow.
Whatever the situation,
your face brings me joy,
your voice brings me pleasure,
and your presence brings me comfort.
Whether joy or sorrow touch my life,
your friendship gives me more than words could ever say.

Remember old friends we've met along the way.
The gifts they've given us stay with us every day.

MARY McCASLIN

ॐ

Friends . . .

they cherish one another's hopes.

They are kind to one another's dreams.

HENRY DAVID THOREAU

I have learned so much from you.
And you taught more by example
than your words ever said.
From your life, I have learned not to say, "If only. . ."
because this phrase speaks of regrets.
I no longer say, "But. . ."
because this one small word relinquishes
responsibility and offers up excuses.
You have taught me that I cannot go back
and change the way I handled the past.
Now I take what life offers,
and I use it for good and growth.
Together we face toward tomorrow, not yesterday.
"If only" and "But" are not in our vocabulary.
Thank you for your example.

❧

The key is to keep company with people who uplift you,
whose presence calls forth your best.

ELIZABETH WILLET

This communicating of a person's self to a friend
works two contrary effects;
for it redoubleth joy,
and cutteth griefs in half.

FRANCIS BACON

Grief can take care of itself,
but to get the full value of joy you must have somebody
to divide it with.

MARK TWAIN

Dear friends, no matter how we find them,
are as essential to our lives as breathing in and breathing out.

LOIS WYSE

❧

*In the plan of God,
a friendship is a touch of
heaven on earth.*

MARK CONNOLLY

❧

I thank God more for friends than for my daily bread—
for friendship is the bread of the heart.

MARY MITFORD

Few delights can equal the mere presence of
one whom we trust utterly.

GEORGE MACDONALD

❧

*A friend may well be reckoned the
masterpiece of nature.*

RALPH WALDO EMERSON

❧

What is a friend? I will tell you.
It is a person with whom you dare to be yourself.

FRANK CRANE

Friends remind us we are part
of something greater than ourselves, a larger world.

BARBARA JENKINS

❧

Sometimes I get so preoccupied with my own life, my own troubles and pleasures and trifling concerns. Left to myself, I'd probably just mill around inside my own head, buzzing in tiny circles like a bee that's caught inside a window.

Thank you for all the times you throw open the window and let that silly bee go free. You let in the fresh air and help me regain my sense of perspective. Your friendship is good for me.

❧

Friends are like windows through which
you see out into the world and back into yourself.

MERLE SHAIN

The heartfelt counsel of a friend is
as sweet as perfume and incense.

PROVERBS 27:9 NLT

❧

Advice is like snow.
The softer it falls,
the longer it dwells and
the deeper it sinks into the mind and heart.

SAMUEL COLERIDGE

❧

Where would I be without you?
When I think of all the times
I've called you up to ask your advice,
all the times you've dropped what you were doing
to listen, to ponder, to pray,
to help me find solutions and new possibilities. . .
all I can say is thank you.

There are no words to express the abyss
between isolation and having one ally.
It may be conceded to the mathematician
that four is twice two,
but two is not twice once; two is two thousand times one.

G. K. CHESTERTON

❧

*When I count my blessings,
I count you.*

3

You Are My Soul Mate

When we first got to know each other, I felt as though something inside of me recognized something inside of you. When I spoke about my thoughts and feelings, you understood. When you described your life, I could relate to what you said. The same things made us laugh. We shared our faith and found a common ground.

I felt as though I had been a stranger in an alien land—but at last I had found someone who spoke the same language I did. I was no longer alone.

One does not make friends.
One recognizes them.

IRENE DUNN

No soul is desolate as long as there is a human
for whom it can feel trust and reverence.

GEORGE ELIOT

⁂

What is a friend?
A single soul in two bodies.

ARISTOTLE

A soul mate is someone to whom
we feel profoundly connected,
as though the communicating and communing
that take place between us
were not the product of intentional efforts,
but rather a divine grace.

THOMAS MOORE

There's something beautiful about finding
one's innermost thoughts in another.

OLIVER SCHREINER

The friend given you by circumstances
over which you have no control was God's own gift.

FREDERICK ROBERTSON

A true friend is the gift of God and. . .
He only who made hearts can unite them.

ROBERT SOUTH

❧

A friend understands what you are trying to say. . .
even when your thoughts aren't fitting into words.

ANN D. PARRISH

❧

Your best friend is the person
who brings out of you the best that is within you.

HENRY FORD

27

Insomuch as any one pushes you nearer to God,
he or she is your friend.

FRENCH PROVERB

❧

My friend shall forever be my friend,
and reflect a ray of God to me.

HENRY DAVID THOREAU

❧

One of the best things about our friendship:
The way you help me draw closer to God.
I see His face in yours.

Friendship, gift of heaven, pleasure of great souls!

VOLTAIRE

◈

A friend is what the heart needs
all the time.

HENRY VAN DYKE

◈

The language of friendship is not words but meaning.

HENRY DAVID THOREAU

$\mathcal{T}o$ practice the art of friendship you need to:

Hear what I do not say,
    See what I cannot see,
        Speak when I need to hear,
            Walk close to my heart,
                Touch my life with your understanding,
                And treasure all we share.

Thank you for never failing to practice these gentle arts.

❦

Friendship:
It involves many things,
but, above all, the power of going out of
one's self and seeing and appreciating whatever is
noble and loving in another.

THOMAS HUGHES

4

My Yesterday
Friend,
My Tomorrow
Friend

When first we met, our skin was creamy, smooth, and firm.
Now crow's feet crinkle the corners of our eyes.
Each line speaks to me of laughter
shared down through the years.

When first we met, we were ready to leap up mountains
and change the world.
Now our gait is slower,
but we still walk in step.

The years may have changed us on the outside.
But our hearts remain the same.
The years have only made our friendship richer.

❧

*To me, fair friend,
you never can be old.*

SHAKESPEARE

No love, no friendship can
cross the path of our destiny
without leaving some mark
on it forever.

FRANCOIS MAURIAC

❧

You have left your mark on my heart.
I am a better person because of you.
I am grateful for the past;
I enjoy our present friendship;
I anticipate the future.
Thank you for your presence in my life.
You are my forever friend.

A knowledge that another has felt as we have felt,
and seen things not much otherwise than we have seen them,
will continue to end to be one of life's choicest blessings.

ROBERT LOUIS STEVENSON

✦

I count myself in nothing else so happy
As in a soul remembering my good friends.

WILLIAM SHAKESPEARE

Come in the evening, or
Come in the morning;
Come when you're looked for,
Or come without warning.

THOMAS O. DAVIS

❧

*Friendships, like geraniums,
bloom in kitchens.*

PETER LORIMER

❧

I will always have time for you.
My door is always open.
And my kitchen table's always waiting
for you to pull up a chair.
You're always welcome!

Only friends will tell you the truths you need to hear to make the last part of your life bearable.

FRANCINE DuPLESSIX GRAY

જ

I'm looking forward
to growing old together!

Some may value their bank accounts,
their professional titles, their homes and property. . .
But when I count the truly valuable things in my life. . .
You're one of the first things on my list!

My friends are my estate.

EMILY DICKINSON

$\mathcal{I}$ consider your friendship to be a sacred gift.
You have been an inspiration to me on my journey of faith.
Our pilgrimage of friendship has led us to unexpected places,
but along the way, you have always be a blessing in my life.
I am grateful for the day I met you,
and I look forward to knowing you
tomorrow
and for eternity.

True friendships are lasting
because true love is eternal.
A friendship in which heart speaks to heart
is a gift from God.

HENRY NOUWEN

℘

When you're with a friend,
your heart has come home.

EMILY FARBER

Thank you for. . .

long talks;
understanding smiles;
taking time to be with me;
shared laughter;
prayer.

I'm glad we're friends!